The Oracle's Guide

Dream Interpretation
VOLUME 1 and VOLUME 2

BY MPHO KHOZA

The oracle's guide
To dream interpretation

Volume 1
Interpretation of dreams

Book 1

What are dreams?

Why do dreams need to be interpreted?

How do we accurately interpret dreams?

What are the benefits of dream interpretation?

Book 2

Types of dreams

Lucid dreams

Natural and universal dreams

Nightmares

Book 3

Symbolism

Animal dreams

Water dreams

Colors, material and objects in your dreams

Characters in your dream (human beings, ETs , Robots, machines, dogs, birds, lions, fishes, hyenas, cats, etc.)

Introduction

Volume one of The Oracle's Guide to Dream interpretation consists of five important aspects of your dreams, which appear in almost every dream you have when you are sleeping. In this version (Book 1, 2 and 3)   I will explain each category and give a guide to how you should interpret such dreams and how to understand their meanings in your everyday life. I have a unique understanding of how dreams work and what they mean to us as dreamers, though most people use spiritual guides and religious books to interpret dreams. Some go to the extent of using scientific methods to explain dreams while others go the astrological way. As The Oracle (*notice that I didn't say* 'as an Oracle "this I explain in my biography) I make my interpretations as simple as I can for even a toddler to understand. Because it is my duty to simplify the complicated matrix of our dreams which affect our daily lives. I have a gift to be a guide to those who are lost in the confusion of the hidden and the unknown mysteries of the spiritual worlds. My interpretations are not influenced by religion or any believe system, culturally, spiritually or scientifically. However there may be similarities in my interpretations to those of various believe systems but that will be a coincidence or a confirmation of my words to those who believe in the same things as it may confirm certain truths in their believe systems.

Volume 1 will be followed by other volumes of similar content which will be **The Oracle's guide** to other aspects like, ***The guide to traditional healer's initiation, The guide to Healing yourself, The guide to living without fear, The guide to use***

colored candles and ***The guide to seeing into the future, etc.***
These books will follow each other in no particular sequence.

Volume 1 of **The Oracle's guide to dream interpretation** will
be followed by other Books which will be explaining in detail
each category of dreams and breaking down each dream's
meanings.

Other volumes of **The Oracle's Guide** will focus on traditional
healing and indigenous Shamanic practices as well as future
predictions by The Oracle himself. If you are interested in
learning the secrets of spirituality and looking for a guide to
open up your third eye these are the books you should read.

The Oracle's guide
BOOK 1

Interpretation of Dreams

What are dream?

DREAMS are random replays of stored memories and extractions of events forgotten which happens almost every minute and second of our lives in our subconscious minds. We are blessed with the ability to see things with our open eyes and even with our eyes closed. The physical reality we experience with our five senses we also experience in our imaginations/dreams. Our imaginations/dreams can travel through vast realities and reach beyond any boundaries of space and time. Though our nature as human beings allows us limited access to everything our imaginations can conceive. We also carry the ability of receiving information from other realms of reality. We possess five senses in our physicality which are, touch, smell, taste, hearing and sight. But beyond our physicality in the spirit form we possess even more senses which are the advanced versions of the physical five and more. These senses include love, compassion, trust, intuition and what we call conscience. All of these nonphysical senses can be utilized consciously or unconsciously, depending on the state or situation you find yourself in.

 We have a place where we store information as memory, a place where anything is made possible by the power of imagination. In this place we are able to visualize the past, present and the future. Our brain is an organ that houses this place called the Mind; all experiences are stored and processed there. But where do dreams fit in in this brain? Which part of our brain is responsible for housing dreams?

We are told in scientific terms that dreams are made of information stored in our subconscious mind where the information is extracted when our bodies are in a resting mode. When we dream, certain cells in our brains are in a state where they function without disturbance as other cells would be switched off or in a resting mode. It is therefore a way of unpacking and restructuring of information that is stored in our subconscious mind, Information that comes to live when we are asleep or in a deep relaxed mode. To tap into the dream world can mostly be achieved through sleeping, but some people can visit these worlds even in their wake state through meditation or deep thinking. Imagination can sometimes be dubbed as day dreaming as you would be hallucinating or be day dreaming while you are awake. Science explains in detail how the chemicals in our brains balances themselves out by filing and categorizing information in sections and segments built and designed for specific categories. This is where you have your memory stored in its place and senses functioning with commands from other parts of your brain. There are scientific names for those parts of your brain, but since this is not a Biology or Science book. I will not bore you with the names and scientific explanations. Besides, I am not a scientist and I have little knowledge in those fields of study. However as The Oracle I know well the spiritual side of our physical being than the biological side.

Spirituality teaches us that dreams are a channel that can lead us to tap into other worlds and other universes. The supernatural and mystic realms are associated with dreams according to different cultural believe systems and religious views. Since the beginning of human existence, dreams have served as a sanctuary and a haven for troubled minds or as a hell to unknowing minds. People have been dreaming and imagining their realities before they could even experience them. In some culture's folklores it is told that the universe was created out of something's or someone's imagination. Which means something or someone dreamed about the universe before it existed then the universe came to be out of that dream. So the importance of dreams among us as human beings derives from believing that everything was created from an imagination or a dream. We also believe that existence doesn't end in physicality only but there are other realms of existence which we cannot experience through our physicality. Hence there are believes of the afterlife and the before life.

In this volume I am going to explain in detail what dreams are and what they mean to your everyday life experiences. This is a step by step guide to interpretation of dreams. Other extended explanations may be found in the upcoming volumes of this version.

Dreams are not real - this is a true statement which can be backed up by facts which are based on the understanding of reality. Anything that we can experience with our physical senses we dub as real. We believe in the physical world as reality because we can see, smell, taste and touch it. What we cannot see, smell, taste or touch is imaginary or supernatural to us. And those unseen instances depending on one's believes can be either true or false. It takes a certain degree of convincing for one to instill his believes onto others. But once convinced, people can go to greater lengths to protect what they believe.

The truth of the matter is, what you believe may differ from what I believe but neither of us may be wrong or right.

The purpose of dreaming – can be categorized as unconscious desires and wishes which are stored somewhere in our forgotten storages. It can also be the way for our brains to interpret random signals from our bodies while we sleep. And most importantly dreaming can work as a form of psychotherapy. Where in spiritual believes it can be a way for humans to interact with the spirit world.

The spiritual side of dreams - in the spiritual world there are many dimensions which exist in deferent realms. There are spiritual beings and entities which coexist with the physical world. Everything in existence is connected whether spiritual or physical. We were created by spiritual energies and became spiritual beings living in the physical body. Everything that happens in the physical has already happened in the spiritual. We can feel and explain the physical through science and other methods of understanding the physical existence. And we can also feel and explain the spiritual world through consciousness, intuition and dreams. Or by opening your third eyes (this shall be explained in detail on the next book) ,

Why do dreams need to be interpreted?

For us to understand where we are going we need to understand where we come from and tap into the future with our imaginations to prepare ourselves for the coming events. Dreams are our guides through life; they warn us or give us signals when we are unaware of certain dangers. They heal our minds and enrich our consciousness with knowledge. Dreams carry important messages from our very own souls to our physical bodies and from our ancestor or our spiritual guides to our learning minds. Certain dreams come as warnings to people, alerting them of the dangers which lie ahead or situations which one needs to avoid.

- ❖ Dreams can also come as reminders of things which you have forgotten, especially those that may be of value to you in future if you remember them. Those who are going through a process of discovering themselves may find their answers in dreams. Psychotherapy may also be achieved through dreams. Prophetic messages may come to those who are gifted through dreams and help other people as well. Healing conditions such as depression can be achieved through dreaming.
- ❖ Shamans often dream of medicinal herbs before they dig them up and mix them to heal people.
- ❖ Gurus and monks use dreams as a gateway to travel to other realms of reality.
- ❖ Dreams may also bring fresh ideas to creative minds

If you do not understand your dreams you will not know what to do with the messages your dreams may bring to you. The importance of interpreting dreams depends on the seriousness of the individuals who receive these dreams and most importantly believing in dreams.

How do we correctly interpret dreams?

Through using guides from your religious teachings or following the words of your Gurus and Oracles, you can learn how to interpret your own dream. Learning the right way to interpret dreams helps us not to confuse real dreams with false dreams or hallucinations.

- ❖ Learn the language of dreams (the symbols and signs in your dreams)
- ❖ Compare the dream to your life experiences
- ❖ Know your desires from your needs and see if your dream was influenced by desire or need
- ❖ Connect with your spirit guides
- ❖ Communicate with your ancestors
- ❖ Meditate and practice rituals which enable you to remember your dreams
- ❖ Remember your dreams
- ❖ Do not take everything you saw in your dreams literally
- ❖ Know the meanings of animals in your dreams
- ❖ Know the meanings of natural and unnatural objects in your dreams
- ❖ Understand the entities who visit you in your dreams. Know who they are and why they visit you.
- ❖ Understand the signs and symbols in your dreams

If you take your dreams for granted and ignore the signs. If you don't want to remember your dreams, you will always miss the point of your dreams.

What are the benefits of dream interpretation?

Once you are able to interpret your dreams, you will have the power to control your destiny. You will be able to tell when there are certain destructions or dangers coming your way. You will be able to tackle every challenge with the understanding of their effects in the spirit world.

- ❖ You will be warned before danger occurs in your life
- ❖ You will acquire knowledge which you were never taught in the physical world
- ❖ You will get to experience other worlds which only exist in other dimensions
- ❖ Your spirit grows and your consciousness becomes more open to the physical and the spiritual world
- ❖ You can connect with your guides and ancestors through dreams
- ❖ Your gifts or abilities will be enhanced
- ❖ Some healing of the body, mind and soul occur in dreams
- ❖ Understanding of life and purpose will be easy
- ❖ You can help others through what you learn from your dreams

Interpretation of Dreams

Types of dreams

Lucid dreams are caused by signals sent by the subconscious mind to the body from the space and time framed files. While you are falling into a sleep state your brain continues to function in a wake state. Such dreams have deeper meanings as the meanings are scripted in the feelings and emotions which were created when some events occurred in your wake state. Your brain replays the events in your sleep while you respond to them in reality. These will feel like dejavu, where certain events seems familiar sometimes feeling like you've been there before. They often feel as real as in your wake state.

- ❖ Some call lucid dreams sleep walking, where else the walking seldom happens in certain events but the physicality and realism of the dream leaves the dreamer with wonders and astonishment. This may occur when the dreamer is overwhelmed with stress and confusion in matters of spirituality or life in general.
- ❖ Sometimes visitations from other entities happen in such dreams, where you find yourself connecting with strange beings or finding yourself in strange lands and spaces. Ancestors also appear in such dreams as messengers or

gift bearers where the dreamer can touch and feel their presence.

- Most of the time when you wake up from these dreams you will feel the after effects of the events which happened in that dream. The severity and intenseness of the feelings will tell how important the dream was.
- In other cases witchcraft may be involved, where evil creatures are sent to cast spells on you. Sometimes fighting with you or forcing things down your throat.
- Such instances where creatures are sent to you will leave you with physical scars or internal pains. Similar to when you have been bewitched and a sickness spell has been cast on you, immediately when you wake up you start to feel sick.
- It may be that nothing entered your home physically but spiritually something would have entered which will affect your physical body.
- Warning signs are there in these dreams and shouldn't be taken lightly as they normally are the last warnings before something drastic occurs.
- But these dreams are not always as bad as I have mentioned, sometimes they come in good faith.
- You may find yourself walking out of your bed towards something which needs your attention. Or find yourself interacting with a good spirit guide who wishes to connect you with something very important in your life.
- Some lucid dreams are just as silly as our thinking. You'd find yourself holding something only to wake up with the exact thing in your hand. That would be your subconscious mind telling you about the things that are happening to you at that moment while you sleep.

Natural and universal dreams – occur on a daily basis, some are influenced by our earlier thought while some happen randomly. I call them natural dreams because they happen naturally and they happen every day even though we don't remember some of them. It has been proven by scientists that every living being dreams in their sleep twice or thrice a night or day. Natural dreams are some of the dreams which occur every time we are asleep.

- ❖ They serve as a mind refresher and psychotherapy to sick people.
- ❖ They are mostly the recollection of thoughts and experiences which passed before you slept.
- ❖ Natural dreams can also mimic the things that are happening around you while you sleep.
- ❖ Sometimes you'll hear someone calling you in a dream where else someone would be calling you in reality.
- ❖ Sound, smell and touch are often felt in natural dreams as they occur in reality.
- ❖ Such dreams may also carry messages and warnings which you already thought of in your wake state but needed clarity on them.
- ❖ In those instances your brain will be clarifying or reassuring you of your doubts and wonders.
- ❖ You may dream of your deceased relatives or loved ones, but that may not necessarily be a message or a warning. That would be your mind missing that person or a process of healing from your loss.
- ❖ Natural dreams can mix lucid dreams and nightmares at once, and they can be as confusing as any other complex dream.

Nightmares – are terrifying dreams which sometimes occur like lucid dreams. They often feel as real as in a wake state and have the tendency to paralyze our bodies when they attack. Sleeping paralysis is one of the descriptions given to these dreams as they have a tendency of paralyzing the dreamers in their sleep. These dreams mostly occur when we are sleeping in an uncomfortable positions or when we are too relaxed in our sleep. Our bodies are built in such a way that everything that happens to them gets registered in the mind. Your mind will react to any discomfort on the body even when you are asleep. That is why most of our nightmares are caused by discomfort. But thoughts can also play a role in sleep paralysis, like after watching a horror movie or after witnessing a horrible event. Even bad news may cause nightmares and in such occurrences nightmares may occur as natural dreams or lucid dreams given the influencing factor of that dream. Nightmares occur in all forms of dreams as long as there is discomfort or stress in both your body and mind.

- ❖ Muscle pulls can cause sleeping paralysis
- ❖ Tiredness can also cause sleep paralysis
- ❖ Evil spirits and dark creatures may cause nightmares.
- ❖ Sometimes certain energies may affect your sleep and cause nightmares, like the room you are sleeping in. if that room is filled with negative vibrations nightmares are likely to occur
- ❖ If someone with negative energy stands next to you while you are sleeping a nightmare may occur

- ❖ If an owl or crow lands on top of your house while you sleep they may cause nightmares.(this will be discussed in detail when we unpack animal meanings in dreams)
- ❖ Children also have nightmares when there are negative energies around the area where they sleep
- ❖ Timid people can easily get nightmares as they are easily frightened, mostly when they dream about snakes and other frightening animals.
- ❖ Messages carried in nightmares are normally regarded as warning signs.

Other volumes of The Oracles guide … will go into detail on matters regarding dreams and the animals which appear in them. Especially when I will be discussing issues pertaining spirituality and Shamanism. These are summaries of vast details on dreams and the symbols which occur in those dreams.

Interpretation of Dreams

Symbolism- these are the entities, objects, shapes, colors and animals which occur in your dreams. They serve as message codes which tell the story behind the story that you see in your dream. The irony of the dream is embedded in these symbols, therefore it is imperative to understand these symbols and be able to decipher them. Interpretation of dreams delves mostly on these parts of your dreams. There are different types of symbols and different meanings for each dream. Knowledge and understanding of these symbols will enable you to interpret your dreams according to what they mean to you and what they mean in your life.

Geometric shapes show your mental state and the space you are occupying at present. They also show time, the time it will take for something to happen if your dream is a warning or the time it took for you to realize the importance of certain things in your life. Geometric shapes also represent a plan, a plan that you can use to tackle certain issues or a plan for the future. This helps a lot when one is a business man or a strategic worker. The accuracy of these symbols is a sign of things going well and plans being approved by your spirit guides. But the inaccuracy will show the opposite, where things may not go well or plans which were not thoroughly researched and incorrectly implemented. Certain geometric shapes represent structures that you will be involved in or structures which you will build. Artists often have these dreams as an enhancement of creativity or the degrading of one's talent. A clear understanding of these shapes and their meaning will help in interpreting such dreams. I will go int detail when I explain each shape and its meaning on the next volume.

Colors may vary in terms of places and objects in those dreams. But they play a pivotal role in distinguishing the warning signs and the future predictions. They also make you aware of the bearers of the message as different spirits and entities bring messages to you. Some people do not dream in color, their dreams appear in black and white or in total darkness. That also has a very important meaning to that person's life. People with spiritual gifts often have both black and white as well as colorful dreams. The trick is to understand the meaning of such dreams and being able to decipher the story behind the dream.

Voices –sometimes we hear voices in our dreams but not seeing where they derive from or the source of those voices. Sometimes we speak to people whom we can see but their words come from outer space, you'd hear their voices but their mouths wouldn't be making any movements. Those are spiritual dreams; our guides use such dreams to deliver important spiritual messages to us. Details of such will be found in THE ORACLE'S GUIDE TO SELFHEALING and THE ORACLE'S GUIDE TO INNITIATION. Both volumes contain detailed information about such dreams.

Animal dreams – animals are totem symbols in certain indigenous cultures as well as certain spiritual organizations. Animals play a very important role when it comes to spiritual dreams because they always come as a warning to the dreamer. These dreams should never be ignored because of the significance and the seriousness of the messages they carry. When your spirit guides or ancestors visit you they will sometimes disguise themselves as animals. The color of the animal and the state of being are the most important aspects which must be considered when it comes to interpreting such dreams. Every animal represents a spiritual entity or a situation in your life. Deciphering such dreams will open doors where difficulties are met and will also guide you in the direction you should take for whatever reason you may be in need of.

Four legged animals' represents living things; your enemies, your family and friends, your livestock and your associates are depicted as such animals. Here and there you will find spirits which are represented by such animals but that would depend on the type of animal and the color of that animal. For instance; a black dog may represent your enemies while a brown dog may represent your ancestors. White dogs are a different story too which will also be covered in volume 2. But you should pay attention to what happens in your dreams especially when animals are involved because they carry different meanings for different folks. When animals attack in a dream it is a different story to when they come in peace.

Reptiles and sea creatures represent the water spirits and they also represent the past and the future. Here also the colors of these animals play a pivotal role in the messages they carry. Fishes are often associated with spiritual gifts and birth or life giving sources. Snakes and lizards are associated with ancestors or other entities from other universes. Understanding the behavior of such animals in their habitats may help you decipher the message behind such dreams as they often behave strange when they appear in dreams.

There are many animals which appear in our dreams and each carry a different meaning.

Birds are animals which always carry messages whether good or bad it will depend on the type of bird you will be dreaming about. But birds are message bearers and they represent messengers or beings that are always sent to deliver messages. Details of these too are in volume 2. It will help the dreamer so much to understand each bird and its message so that interpretation of those messages may not be confused. The types of birds which carry good messages are those that are good looking and sometimes colorful. But bad messages are often brought by eagles, vultures and owls. One should be able to tell when the message is bad; such dreams are frightening and sometimes leave you with unpleasant feelings.

Water dreams – these are body, mind and spiritual dreams. They bring awareness and knowledge of spirituality as well as physical healing. Water is for purification and cleansing and sometimes healing. Water dreams may alert you about certain things that you are neglecting in your life. It may also be a sign that something needs to be done to cleanse your body or your soul. These dreams may also show you the direction in which you need to take through your spiritual journey or through your initiation process. I speak widely about this on THE ORACLE'S GUIDE TO INITIATION.

- ❖ The sign that one needs to be cleansed often comes in a form of water
- ❖ When healing is required in one's body or soul water will appear in your dreams
- ❖ When you have to undergo initiation as a Shaman or traditional healer water will appear in your dreams but the irony is in how the water appears and what happens in that dream when water is involved. Not every water

dream notates the need to be initiated. It is in the signs and happenings of that dream that the message can be interpreted as an initiation process.

- ❖ Water dreams can also appear as nightmares or lucid dreams where you wake up wet to the core. In a case where the dreamer is depressed, there may be scenes of drowning or being carried away by drifting water. But one shouldn't fear such dreams because they carry very important messages especially messages connected to the dreamer's spiritual journey.

Water creatures such as Mermaids may also appear giving you objects or talking to you. Such are very highly spiritually motivated dreams which should never be ignored as they may be good or very bad dreams. The messages in those dreams will sometimes require a Shaman or The Oracle to decipher. There might be a need to consult your guides to find answers for such dreams. Details of such dreams are written in THE ORACLE'S GUIDE TO INITIATION.

Characters in your dream – winged beings, dead people, spirits, mysterious creatures and imaginary entities are often visitors in our dreams. Some of these dreams are as ridiculous as the science fiction movies we watch on TV. But not all of them are as ridiculous, they may be as important as any spiritual dream depending on the message carried in that dream and the seriousness of the situation depicted in that dream. Some of these dreams are a figment of our imaginations while others are true visitations from spiritual entities. The dreamer needs to understand the characters that are visiting and their intensions. Many people are deceived by such dreams and get the wrong interpretation therefore getting lost in their way of life. Some of these beings may be representing you while they are talking to you. Such a dream would be showing you what you are supposed to say or what you are supposed to think. Or it would be showing you what you said and how it was received. These are some of the aspects which confuse many dreamers. I have dedicated a whole book on this subject where I explain self-healing and self-discovery, this book details how much we are connected to the spirit and how woven everything can intertwine. THE ORACLE'S GUIDE TO SELFHEALING

Dreaming about your dead grandmother or grandfather may not necessarily mean a visitation from your ancestors. Be careful when you interpret such dreams because even negative entities may appear as familiar faces, to influence you to participate in their negative agenda. Your guides or ancestors will never ask you to do evil, unless if you yourself are an evil person therefore your dreams may be influenced by your evilness. A mind sees what it chooses to see, it is the same in dreams. Your character also plays a role in the type of dreams you have.

Winged beings or angelic beings mostly appear to religious and spiritual people depending on what they mean to the person's believe system. Such beings carry messages of peace and prosperity. Some people who believe in luck regard these dreams as signs of fortune and prosperity. But that is a matter of opinion, as The Oracle I can assure you the truth is in the eyes of the beholder. You are saved and healed by your believe.

Extraterrestrial beings are contemporary stories that are roaming our minds since the UFO sightings and the TV shows. Lately Dreamers find themselves encountering these beings in their dreams. It doesn't mean people never dreamed of them in ancient times, it is just that those dreams were not as popular as they are today. Such dreams have existed since the beginning of man's encounter with space beings. It has nothing to do with portals opening in space or abduction experiences. These dreams are as important as any other dream, the trick is how to decipher and interpret them. The Oracle has a short story on these beings which will soon be released in other volumes of THE ORACLE'S GUIDE.

ET's carry messages of wisdom, initiation and spiritual gifts. Those too can bring good or bad to a dreamer depending on their spiritual experiences.

Conclusion

This volume was a summary of almost all the books that are linked in the series of THE ORACLE'S GUIDE. A new volume will be released after every two months in sequel until all volumes are published. More books will follow in different categories as THE ORACLE'S GUIDE..

May the wisdom of your guides continue to nourish your mind and the loves of your ancestors continue to warm your heart.

Until the next volume ASHE !!!

Upcoming Volumes of The Oracle's Guide

Volume 2 Interpretation of dreams

Volume 3 The signs and symbols in dreams

Volume 4 The guide to Shaman initiation

Volume 5 The guide to healing yourself

Volume 6 The guide to living without fear

Volume 7 The guide to use colored candles

Volume 8 The guide to seeing into the future

Volume 9 Understanding spiritual entities

Volume 10 Understanding the higher self

The Author's biography

I am the self-initiated Shaman whose spiritual journey began in 2004, after I was diagnosed with depression. Medical Doctors and Psychologists tried in vain to help me, even traditional healers and prophets failed. At the brink of my condition I attempted suicide but didn't succeed. That's when I started having dreams, dreams of entities from other worlds. In those dreams I had meetings with highly intelligent beings who helped me heal. I was told that depression has no cure but through encounters with these beings I was healed. I was healed spiritually before I could heal mentally. I realized I had a gift when I found ways to selfheal without using any medication. I started using practical methods to keep myself conscious and healthy, even when I encountered challenges in my social life I would automatically come up with methods to resolve any issues effortlessly. Through dreams and meditation all of that was achieved.

I came to realize the importance of the dreams I was having, and taught myself how to interpret them through applied experiences. Thanks to meditation I evolved spiritually, to a point where solutions just came to me without me asking. Some of the people closest to me realized this gift too. They came asking for advice and interpretation of their dreams. Seeing that my help was working well for them, they started referring other people to me for such help. People were healed without medicine. Other people consulted their guides through me. That's where I got the tittle or the nick name of The Oracle. They compared me to the character on The Matrix movie, the character that had the ability to see into the future. Since then I have been helping a lot of people and evolving as a spiritual guide and a healer.

I started writing in 2018 after I had a revelation which I will share in the near future on my upcoming books. Though I never got a chance to acquire educational degrees and literary skills, the little knowledge I have and through practice helped me to jot down what you are reading now. I was able to jot down a few lines to express what has been gifted to me. I hope these volumes will be of great help to those who are in need of the information within. If not enough has been said in these written words, I can still be reached on various platforms of social media and contact channels such as emails and telephone.

May the peace of your spirit fill your body with harmonious energy that allows you to selfheal and self-initiate.

The oracle's guide
To
dream interpretation

Volume 2
Deciphering the symbols

By Mpho Khoza

TABLE OF CONTENTS

Introduction

BOOK 1

Geometric symbols

- ➢ **Square shapes**
- ➢ **Triangles**
- ➢ **Circles**
- ➢ **Diamonds**
- ➢ **Architectural structures**

BOOK 2

Animal symbols

- ➢ **Birds**
- ➢ **Four legged mammals**
- ➢ **Reptiles**
- ➢ **Sea creatures and fish**
- ➢ **Insects**

Water

- ➢ **Rivers and oceans**
- ➢ **Underground water**
- ➢ **Stable water/Dams**
- ➢ **Rain**
- ➢ **Tap water**

BOOK3

Material objects and machines

> - Money and jewelry
> - Cars and houses/buildings
> - Computers and Artificial intelligence
> - Flying machines and UFOs
> - Clothing and garments

BOOK 4

Colors

> - Red
> - Black
> - Green
> - Blue
> - White
> - Yellow
> - Brown
> - Other colors

Conclusion

Introduction

Dream interpretation can prove to be difficult when one lacks the understanding of the symbols depicted in their dreams. In Volume 1 of The Oracle's Guide to Dream Interpretation we discussed the importance of dream interpretation and the key symbols which make your dreams relevant to interpretation, and the value of dreaming.

Volume 2 is the continuation of the previous volume with the breaking down of symbols and the meanings there of. This version will go into detail while taking you step by step into the technique of interpreting dreams, and understanding the deep spiritual meaning of your dreams.

In the spiritual world there are many dimensions which exist in deferent realms. There are spiritual beings and entities which coexist with the physical world. These spiritual entities we cannot see with our naked or physical eyes. But not all are invisible to our naked eyes; some make appearances here and there when it's necessary. They appear in our wake state and in lucid dreams which we explained in volume 1 of The Oracle's Guide to dream interpretation.

In a case of spiritually enlightened people or the gifted ones, these entities are a normal sight as it may be in everyone else's. Everything in existence is connected whether spiritual or physical. We were created by spiritual energies and became spiritual beings living in the physical body. Everything that happens in the physical has already happened in the spiritual. We can feel and explain the physical through science and other methods of understanding the physical existence. And we can also feel and explain the spiritual world through consciousness, intuition and dreams.

In dreams we find senseless events and senseless occurrences which sometimes appear as silly figments of our imaginations. We sometimes resent the notion of dreams when we compare them to reality. Dreaming becomes less important especially when those meaningless dreams do not add value to our daily challenges. Dreamers often see their dreams as a waste of sleep and thieves of their resting time. Some people want to rest all parts of their bodies when they are sleeping; including their minds. It is annoying to have a dream disturbing your rest while you didn't invite any of it. Hence some people do not even care whether they dream or not. While some people who believe in dreams find it stressing when they can't remember their dreams or when they can't seem to tell what the symbolism of their dreams meant.

 Not all dreams may be meaningless and boring, some are interesting with events that entertain as well as excite the dreamer. But the importance of dreaming lies more on the spiritual guidance than the entertainment side. We as spiritually connected people know these sides of dreams but we do not force people to believe or to follow what we teach about dream interpretation. If it works for you follow it whole heartedly but if it doesn't don't force it to, because you will end up confused and confusion is the mother of all stresses in life.

This volume deals with symbols that appear in your dreams as a metaphor to what the dream means to you. Animals and other symbols like geometric shapes and object are the fundamental codes of your spiritual dreams, thus we are going to discuss the meaning of their presence in your dreams.

Step by step you will be guided into the symbolism of your dreams and aspects of your dreams will be unpacked and explained. However there may be censorship in explanations due to the respect of other people's believes and avoiding blasphemes against different religious views.

The aim of this book is to highlight the important parts of your dreams which carry symbolisms in your life experiences. We do not intend to instill any believes in people and we don't force anyone to take the contents of this book as the ultimate truth. Reading with an objective mind will help the reader to not feel offended by the views of the author.

The views and contents of this book are that of the author and none from the publication organization or the government of the country in which the author reside in. all material and contents of the book were derived from the author's perspective and research nothing was stolen or plagiarized from other sources.

I hope every dreamer finds the meanings of the symbols useful in interpreting their dreams. May the guidance of The Oracle be the shining light in your dreams and may you find the contents in this book useful.

BOOK 1

Geometric symbols

Every aspect of our lives dealings and workings are governed by planning, without a plan our endeavors tend to fail. Every day we are faced with unpredictable challenges, which we deem inevitable when they were not foreseen. We have the desire to see things before they happen because we are inquisitive and curious beings, who are infected with fear of the unknown the moment we set foot on earth. Therefore we require careful adjustments when growing and learning especially when it comes to easing the fear of the unknown in our minds. And we can only achieve that through planning.

But how do you plan for something you do not know?

How do you plan for the future that you are uncertain of?

This is where geometric symbols play a role in our dreams.

The accuracy of these symbols is a sign of things going well and plans being approved by your spirit guides. But the inaccuracy will show the opposite, where things may not go well or plans which were not thoroughly researched and incorrectly implemented. Certain geometric shapes represent structures that you will be involved in or structures which you will build. Artists often have these dreams as an enhancement of creativity or the degrading of one's talent. A clear understanding of these shapes and their meaning will help in interpreting such dreams. Geometric symbols often appear in dreams which are enlightening and dreams that are foretelling the future.

The following geometric shapes which appear in your dreams help you to predict the coming events in your life and they also help in restructuring your planning if they are correctly interpreted. Interpretation of these symbols will help you see into your own future like an Oracle.

> **Square shapes**
>
> Square shapes appear in your dreams when things are about to be leveled out. In most cases you will find yourself seeing square shaped objects with writings in them or colors which are bright and luminous.
>
> This would mean that the future looks bright and some of the things in your life; which you might have been planning will be fulfilled.
>
> However, there might be instances where you dream being trapped in a square shaped box or room. That would mean that you are trapped in a plan that you trust but isn't going to work out well for you.
>
> When we imprison ourselves in plans which are straining and draining our mental health, such dreams appear as a warning to a dreamer. A warning that you should change your plan or revisit your thoughts and free yourself from the stress.
>
> In spiritual terms, square shapes will show you that your spirit is complete and content with the situation you are in physically. Square shapes have no negative symbolism in spiritual meanings. They can only show the extent of your spiritual powers and the balancing of spirit and mind.

When you are facing challenges with your spiritual work and looking for solutions. Square shapes may appear as a sign that enlightenment is on the way.

Your spiritual guides will show you square shape or cubes with messages in them to prepare you for the coming enlightenment or the coming transitions in your life. However; if there are no written words or numbers in those cubes, you will see colors which are luminous. Those colors will show you the hidden message behind the cube shape.

Once you've learned how to interpret colors, you will know how to combine the shapes and colors and interpret the message thereof.

➢ **Triangles**

Pyramids and other spiritual structures are built in triangular shapes for the sake of the balancing of energies and the signal connections from the lower realm to the higher realm; from earth to the universe.

Triangles are three sided yet equal on all three sides. This tells us that all three fundamental aspects of your existence are equally important. Body, mind and soul are the most important parts of you as a being; which must be equally respected and equally cared for.

The same applies to the balance of life which is nature, spirit and dimensions. Mother, father and child are also included in these symbols.

When a dreamer sees triangular shapes in their dreams the above mentioned aspects should be considered, that is

the equivalence in the trinity of all things. Such dreams
compel you to look at things in three ways but equally.
 Such dreams depict your life as a perfect balance if all
three are equally cared for or equally nourished.
 If any trinity of your life is not balanced the triangles in
your dream will appear changing shape or crumbling.
Building structures which appear in triangular shapes
depict the holiness or the divinity of such a dream. Your
spiritual guides will be talking to you, showing you what
is needed in your spiritual growth.
Colors which appear in a triangle shape are often warning
signs about your spiritual wellness.
You should consider consulting your Oracle to get a clear
communication with your guides when you see colors
like yellow, white, red or black.
 Normally these colors together with triangles will be a
sign that you have a spiritual calling.
A combination of these colors in a triangle would be a
serious warning that need not be ignored as one might get
ill or encounter danger in the near future.

> **Circles**

Circles symbolize the continuation of things; or the
repetition of the same things starting over and over again.
 Circles will mostly appear to people who are stressed as
a sign of psychotherapy or an alert for one to consider
healing.
 Circles are very highly spiritual shapes; they symbolize
the spirit itself and creation at large.
 All circular shapes are rich in energy and are deep
influencers of the spirit world. When a dreamer is

stressed and the stress affecting their spirituality, circles will appear in their dreams.

When we say your spiritual guides or your ancestors are talking to you specifically circles would have appeared in your dreams.

In situations where problems keep coming in your life and you can't seem to find the solution. You will have circle dreams and those dreams will keep coming back until a solution is found. This means the repetition of troubles in your life which aren't being resolved. Also in such instances you should consult your Oracles for help.

For spiritually gifted people circles represent the eternal life which continuously brings power to the gifted ones. The past present and future are represented in this symbol of eternity.

➢ **Diamonds**

Diamonds mostly appear when the dreamer is felling trapped in a situation which wasn't planned properly. These may appear as crystal diamonds or as a drawing, irrespective of where and how they appear in a dream. As long as it's a diamond shape, confusion will be part of the meaning of that symbol. It will show the confusion in your life and the frustrations you have by confusing you even more.

Your diamond dreams are often confusing and unclear. This should alert you that your life is in turmoil or your confusion is causing problems in your life. Therefore you should consider counseling or communication with your guides.

You may dream of a diamond ring and see it as a sign of marriage as many people do but that is not the case. If marriage is underway, there might be a longing for something else but marriage.

Confusion within the relationship also appears in a form of a diamond ring. This means you should look deep into your relationship and ask yourself if you are doing the right thing.

Do not jump into conclusions when you dream about diamond rings or any jewelry for that matter.

Jewelry in a dream is often an illusion of what is really going on in your life.

Details of jewelry dreams will follow when I discuss objects in your dreams.

Consider diamonds as they are roughly shaped yet equally cut in to size, and then look at your life in that perspective.

> **Architectural structures**

When all of these geometrical shapes appear in a form of an architectural structure, you should consider the meaning of the shape first and place the symbolism of that shape on the building. This means what happens in the shape of the building will actually happen to you in the same meaner and order as it happens in your dream.

In a case where you see someone else in that dream and not yourself, that person should be warned about the coming events.

Shapes in building structures often talk to us in a metaphorical way. The message behind these shapes is of a clustered nature or a closed situation.
In a case where the structure is big and spacious it means your opportunities are vast and unlimited. And in a spiritual meaning that would notate that your spiritual space is open and wide enough for you to let in new energies.

Always remember to interpret such dreams as metaphors and compare the structures to yourself as a being. Circular shaped structures often symbolize sacred places, places of warship or places of spiritual practices. Such dreams would show the need to visit such a place for spiritual revival.

Schools, universities or learning halls and libraries are a symbol of initiation or the need to research and learn certain things in your life which are imperative to your culture or values.

One needs to understand the importance of certain building structures within their cultural use, which would help the dreamer to understand the symbolism of those structures in their dreams especially when they are related to the importance of such structures.

BOOK 2
Animal symbols

Animals represent your spirit guides or your ancestors; some may represent your enemies while others may represent your soul. Since these are living things their symbolism has to do with the living things around you.

In many African cultures animals are symbols of their totems and also represent some surnames. Such totem animals are very important when they appear in your dreams because they speak to your DNA. Your ancestors represent themselves with the pride of their surnames or their totem animals. Animal dreams are mostly messages from your ancestors or your spirit guides.

Sometimes it may be visits from other entities from other realms of existence but those are rare as such entities often represent themselves in their true nature. When it comes to interpreting animal dreams, each animal carries its own symbolism. Understanding each animal's nature will help you to interpret those dreams at ease as these animal's characters play a pivotal role in revealing the messages they carry.

The natural habitats of such animals and the behavioral patens of such animals will also add to the understanding of their symbolism.

The following are some of the animals which commonly appear in our dreams.

> **Birds**
>
> In the dream world birds are called the sky messengers or winged messengers for they are flying entities who bring messages to us the none flying beings.
>
> The messages may be good or bad, pleasant or sad depending on the type of winged creature which delivers the message.
>
> Since birds are messengers, the bearers of good news are those that are colorful and peaceful in nature; Doves, Mocking birds, Flamingos, Parrots and others. These birds appear in your dreams when your guides are bringing good news to you.
>
> Pay attention to the events of that dream as everything that happens in that dream would be a sign of good things to come.
>
> The colors of these birds will also tell how great the pleasantness of the message is. The brighter the color the greater the goodness.
>
> The bearers of bad news are Owls, Falcons, Eagles and Vultures. These are dangerous birds in real life and their nature is not as friendly towards others as the nature of mocking birds and doves.

If one of these birds appears to be attacking you in your dreams it means someone is busy attacking you or they are planning an attack on you.

 The color of the bird is also important because they tell the depth of the message. If the bird is of a dark color it means the warning or the message is intense.

Such dreams require an understanding of colors and the symbolism of birds, the combination will help greatly in interpreting these dreams.

Sometimes owls are sent to bewitch or cast a spell on you; in that case you will dream of it as if it was there in real life. Or you may hear the sound of an owl from outside while you are sleeping. Those are warnings of witchcraft or something bad around your house.
When death is about to enter your family such birds will appear in your dreams, sometimes they will appear taking something from your surroundings or you will see such a bird devouring its prey.

 Those are the signs of death in the family.

- ➢ **Four legged mammals**
  Mammals are totem animals in African cultures; they represent our ancestral lineage and the DNA of an African progeny.
  Dreaming of such animals' means you have a close connection with your ancestors therefore they bring messages to you through such animals.

However, the type of animal and its color thereof are the important parts of your dream. Such characteristics will tell the dreamer what the message is and how to interpret that message.

Domestic animals like cows, goats, sheep and pets like dogs, cats and other small animals are often used by your guides as bearers of spiritual messages.

Dogs are associated with ancestors but only when they are white and brown. If a dog appears in a black color it represents an enemy or a person with negative energy. But in some instances a black dog may represent an angry ancestor depending on what the actual dream entails.

Cats are spiritual animals which are highly respected in African cultures even though some believe they are used by witches for sinister reasons. That is not true, it is arguable in instances where someone has proof but as your guiding Oracle I say it is not true. Cats carry spiritual messages just like dogs.

They represent ancestors and other spiritual entities and they bring strong messages of protection and warnings about the dangers lurking around you.

A cat is like a lion; such dreams depict the protection from your ancestors or the dangers that are coming. That too depends on the color of the cat.

If the cat is dark in color it means danger where else the bright colors mean protection from your ancestors.

Cows are regarded as gods in African spiritual philosophies, which means the highest of the high ancestors or spirit guides. These ancestors are the ones who bring spiritual gifts or a calling.

In most cases your cow dreams will bring messages of initiation into Shamanism or messages of libation practices.

When you have to pay tribute to certain ancestors, cows are used to show you what to do.
In a case where you see a cow being slaughtered it means you must do a certain ritual for your ancestors. However, in some instances the dream may mean that you have to obey certain instructions from your ancestors.

In a case where the cow's color is entirely black the interpretation will differ from those that appear brown or white. That would mean someone being buried in your family. When the cow appears in both black and white color that would mean there is a joining of families in terms of marriage or a communion between ancestors.

Goats are ancestral symbols especially for the spiritually gifted people. When you have a calling you will always dream about goats of all kinds of colors.

A white goat may mean that you have to go for initiation if you have a calling;
Where else a black goat might mean that you have to get rid of bad spirits.
Sometimes even when you do not have a calling; a white goat may depict the fact that you are neglecting your spirit guides. Therefore a ritual is necessary to appease the guides.

Sheep or lamb is the humble animals of our totems which ancestors use when there are joyful ceremonies or thanks giving events.
In a case where you dream about a lamb or sheep that would mean you have to give thanks to your guides and your ancestors.
And in some cases lambs represent the humbleness of one's heart where you need to do introspection and see if you need to humble yourself towards certain situations. Such dreams often guide us towards humble beginnings or a continuation of spiritual humbleness if you are already on that journey.

When animals that are not domesticated like wild elephants and other grass eating mammals appear in your dreams such dreams carry more intense messages than the domesticated animals bring.
In this case you would be dreaming about your health and wellbeing. Wild animals are associated with your body and mind; they bring awareness regarding your health and mental status. In that case your dreams may

come as a warning of an upcoming illness or a sign of depression.

You need to identify the type of animal and its nature to interpret the meaning of such a dream.

In depression cases these animals will appear in distress or appear to be seeking help from you. And in a case where your health is at risk you will see such animals in pain or in a weak state.

The slaughtering of an animal is an indication of libation or honoring your DNA bloodline with some kind of ritual.

- ➢ **Reptiles**

Serpents or belly crawlers or gods of the underworld; which are mostly associated with your guides or species from other realms of our known reality.

Africans believe that reptiles arrived on earth from another planet in the faraway solar system. These creatures arrived here on earth when our ancestors were still primitive and 'uncivilized'. They brought with them technology and wisdom which changed everything our ancestors knew. Many things changed, even our ancestors dreams changed from the way they used to comprehend life.

Many things which were introduced by these beings are still influencing our nature as human beings to this very day. The connection we have with these beings is of a spiritual nature, more on the DNA side as they played a part in advancing our nature as a species.

Dreaming of serpents is a sign of a connection between the dreamer and the other worldly beings which came a long time ago in our lives.

Such dreams are a sign of a spiritual connection with them and a calling that is different from other callings.

Serpents are your spirit guides, whether good or evil both are represented by these entities.

Your ancestors also appear in a form of serpents but such serpents will not frighten nor harm you in a dream.

Brown snakes are often associated with your ancestors and colorful ones represent the situations in your life. Snakes and lizards serve the same symbolism while crocodiles and other dangerous reptiles represent water spirits especially evil ones. These I will explain on the water dream section.

➢ **Sea creatures and fish**

These creatures are almost similar to the serpents as they have similar characteristics and origins. However the meaning of their symbolism differs from serpents as they serve as water spirits and nothing else.

While serpents serve as ancestors, enemies and life experiences. Water creatures are spirits and spirits only.

Fishes are spirits which lead the way, any situation you find yourself in while you're awake, dreaming about fishes means that your spirit guides are going to lead you through it. Big fish like sharks, whales and dolphins represent your teachers who are your water spirit healers or shaman leaders.

When you have to undergo spiritual initiation under water these big fish will appear in your dreams; Similar to dreams about mermaids which are not realistic and sometimes superstitious, but such dreams entails that initiation must take place.

> **Insects**

Small animals often go unnoticed even in our wake life but their existence is as important as any living creature on earth. And in our dreams they appear too, as pests or creepy crawlies.

If you are one of those people who are uncomfortable around insects, such dreams may not be pleasant for you.

Focusing on the nature of such insects and studying their habitual behavior will help in interpreting insect dreams.

Ants are common in dreams and they often bring messages of hard working and building. When your family needs rebuilding and certain people who were lost be brought back in to the family; ants will appear in your dreams.

Also when you need to gather your positions or save for the future you will see ants behaving in their normal character in your dreams.

Where strange activities occur that would mean chaos and confusion in your life.

Other insects like spiders and crickets will always appear when there is something bothering you which you tend to overlook and hope it disappears without solving it. These pests will remind you that nothing goes unnoticed in the spirit world therefore every trouble must be removed in order to live spiritually free.

Water

> **Rivers and oceans**

Moving water has a high significance in our spirituality as we believe that it washes away all the burdens and filth on our bodies.

Dreaming about moving water means that your body needs cleansing; in terms of literally bathing in the river or getting water from the ocean and use it to wash your body. Sometimes this may come as an instruction from your Shaman after you have consulted about your dream. These are serious dreams which must be interpreted correctly as they carry high spiritual messages.

 The symbolism of sea water in our lives always has to do with our spiritual wellbeing and cleansing.

Considering such facts may help understand the meaning of such waters in your dreams.

I get into much detail about this aspect in The Oracle's Guide to Initiation. In that book I explain the dreams and the process of initiating under water.

 The book will follow soon in the collection of The Oracle's Guide.

➢ **Underground water**
Underground water has natural healing powers and is
more connected to our bodies than any other natural
element.

Our bodies are made up of huge amounts of water which
is what makes us dependent on water in many aspects of
our health.

When a dreamer encounters underground water in their
dream that would mean the dreamer needs healing of
some sort and water may be the source of that healing.
If other people are involved in that dream that would
mean those people are also in need of healing and the
dreamer must help them by acquiring underground water
and give it to them.

Normally such dreams appear to gifted people or
healers. If you are not gifted, you should report such a
dream to your Oracle or Shaman as you may need some
guidance in using that water.

The most important thing to remember about the dream is
where the water came out from and what it looked like;
whether it was clear water or dirty water with mud in it.
In a case where the water is clean that would mean
healing and relief, but if the water appears dirty that
would mean an illness or disease that's coming to you.

If the water appears muddy and dirty you should seek immediate help from your healers as the dream may be warning you about a sickness that is hiding within you or one that is coming in the near future.
So prevention is better than cure.

This may also serve as a guide to self-healing if your dream comes with instructions. Following the instructions may lead to self-healing or healing of others.

> **Stable water/Dams/lakes and swamps**
In these waters we often find creatures like crocodiles and water snakes, these are spirit entities represented as water gods.

Stable water dreams often mean that the dreamer has a spiritual gift but in a case where the water is infested with creatures like crocodiles that would mean a different thing.

Crocodiles and water snakes are enemies of your spirituality; they represent the evil that affects you spiritually.

So in a case where the stable water is infested with such creatures that means your spirituality is under attack by low vibrating entities.

However in a case where the water is clear from these creatures that means you are meeting with your water spirit guides; who may be intending to take you for initiation or who may be showing you the extent of your spiritual powers.

These dreams also need to be treated with caution as they may lead to harm if not interpreted correctly.
People end up hurting themselves trying to fulfill what was in their dreams without understanding the real meaning of their dream.

If a dreamer finds themself drowning in a lake that is an indication of spiritual suffocation, which means the dreamer is drowning in confusion and in depression resulting in your spirit not being at ease.

When the spirit is not well or unhappy dreams of drowning are likely to come to you.
 The dreamer will have to consider meditating or consulting for help as the spirit's unhappiness may cause body illnesses.

➢ **Rain**
Blessings upon blessings are coming or are already happening.

Often rain dreams come when something good is about to happen or already happening. This is a way of making you prepare for the acceptance of what may be coming to you. But in a case where the rain is coming with severe

thunder storms that is a warning that the dreamer must
take care of his or her blessings as they may be taken
away in a stormy situation.

Everything that has to do with your blessings is
represented symbolically by rain.

Bad situations or trouble within the dreamer's life will
be shown as the dreamer encounters heavy rains while in
a dream.

The dreamer may be watching the rain from a secure
place or may be in the rain experiencing difficulties while
trying to get away. That is a sign of situations which will
be heavy on you and may be difficult to run away from,
or you may find yourself trapped in such a situation with
no way out.

This part of water dreams is also explained in detail in
the next book, The Oracle's Guide to Initiation.

➢ **Tap water**
Bottled water or contained water and tap water have the
same symbolic meaning which is in line with the health
of the dreamer.

When you dream about tap water running from the tap or
spilling on the ground that means your health is at risk
and healing in a form of something you drink is required.
This symbolizes the need to ingest liquids for healing.

Contained water is a symbol for medicine, any medication of choice is symbolized by water in a container. More on this aspect will also be found when we discuss Shamanism and traditional medicine, which will be in The Oracle's Guide to self-healing

BOOK 3.
Material objects and machines

None living organisms or objects which are used as tools for our survival as human beings are the things that appear in our dreams when there is a concern about such in our lives.

Whether we lose or gain such materials our dreams uses the very same objects as signs of their presences or their loss.

> **Money and jewelry**
Jewelry such as gold, silver and diamond has a connection with our wealth and possessions.
Their symbolism is based on what we work for and what we are given as fortune.

In a case where jewelry is given to you in a dream that is a sign of certain ''wants' 'being satisfied.
Jewelry is not a need in your life therefore it represents your desires and wants. Thus the symbolism of such will always be based on what you acquire as fortune or what you will lose.

The down side of such a dream is in a case where you dream losing those possessions or someone stealing. That would mean losing everything you own to theft or your negligence. Such dreams have little to do with spirituality, unless there are spiritual entities involved in the mix then you would have a different meaning.

If your spirit guides appear in a dream where jewelry is present that would mean there is a warning from their side regarding such materials.
But jewelry is mostly based on your fortune than spirituality.

The same applies to money; gaining and losing money will be depicted in your dreams where you are literally acquiring or losing it.

These dreams are straight forward and have little metaphors in them. In a case where they appear metaphorically it would be in instances where money and possession are a problem in one's life.
Therefore a consultation may be necessary to get clarity on such matters.

➢ **Cars and houses/buildings**
Auto mobiles and flying machines are a form of transportation on earth where else in the spirit world they represent our travels through different dimensions.

On the other hand things like houses and other building structures represent our homes in the spirit world.
This is where your comfort comes from, in a case where you are going through situations in your life that make you feel alone and abandoned by your guides.

Dreaming about houses will give you a sense of security and belonging.

In a case where you dream about a car, you should pay attention to the color of the car and the meaner in which the car is built.
If it's a big car with many passengers that would mean a transition in to the world of many ancestors who are traveling to a certain direction which you are required to travel in.

When someone who has passed on appears in a car wanting to take you on a ride that would mean they want to take you to the other side where you might be asked to stay or be given a choice to return. In that case if you chose to stay that would be your death on earth. But that is determined by the color of the car and the person in it. Such dreams will need to be interpreted with caution as they may confuse the dreamer. When confusion arises from these dreams make sure you consult your Oracle for clarity and clear interpretation.

Traveling in a vehicle whether flying or on wheels is a symbol of traveling in the spiritual realms. Where the dream takes you is the direction in which your soul is headed. Remember to identify the people in the vehicle and the events that are happening in that dream as those are the tell tales of the message in your dream.

- ➤ **Computers and Artificial intelligence**
  Gadgets are our modern day tools to use for easy access
  to communication and information.
  In the dream world they represent a form of
  communication between us and the ones who are on the
  other side of our reality.

  It may be a symbol of communicating with the ancestors
  but sometimes may be a sign that one needs to
  communicate with their inner self.

  Sometimes we experience dreams which are influenced
  by our thoughts so in many cases when we dream of
  gadgets we would be tapping into our subconscious mind
  and reliving some of our daily experiences.

  Gadget dreams are to be treated like any other dream
  especially when there is little or less confusion in them.
  Look at your concerns and check how they fit in your
  dream, this may be a sign of caring too much about
  gadgets or excessively depending on them.

- ➤ **Flying machines and UFOs**
  Since Hollywood started making science fiction movies
  based on UFO encounters, the topic has become a part of
  our lives and has also created in us an awareness of
  certain encounters we used to overlook.

  This may be the result of figments of our imaginations
  or real encounters depending on the realness and the
  seriousness of the situation.

I would like to advice the dreamer to look deep into the dreams and analyze them thoroughly as they may occur as a result of imagination or hallucination.

However there are real encounters of UFO and real dreams which have significant meaning to the dreamer. But to avoid being called insane one needs to be careful when interpreting such dreams.

Mostly such dreams have no symbolism they just come as they are and represent what they depict in your dream. In such cases an encounter would be an encounter and fiction will remain fiction.

There are other entities which exist in other realms of our reality which we cannot ignore if we believe in their existence. But that is a topic for another book. In a dreams perspective one should consult their Oracle or take the dream as literal as it came.

➢ **Clothing and garments**
What we use to cover our bodies serves as protection, identity and disguise.

When we are able to identify different characters according to their different attire, we are able to tell what they stand for and how they want to be identified.

Our guides often use certain attires when they appear to us to make us aware of the guise they are in or make us aware of what needs to be covered and how it should be covered. The type of clothes we see in our dreams are the type of clothes that we see in our wake state but in a case where a garments is worn and it is foreign to our eyes that would mean we have encountered foreign spirits.

 The symbolism of clothes in a dream is as simple as identity and disguise.
It is up to the dream interpreter to see to it that the dream is interpreted as it is and the attire is used to identify who the messengers are and what they want.

BOOK 4
Colors

Colors can uniquely give identity to anything that can be physically seen. Colors may vary in terms of places and objects that appear in those dreams. Colors also play a pivotal role in distinguishing the warning signs and the future predictions as well as the messages there of. They also make you aware of the bearers of the message as different spirits and entities bring messages to you in different colors and shapes.

Some people do not dream in color, their dreams appear in black and white or in total darkness. That also has a very important meaning to that person's life. People with spiritual gifts often have both black and white as well as colorful dreams.

The trick is to understand the meaning of such dreams and being able to decipher the symbolism behind the dream.

> **Red**
>
> We are often told that Red stands for danger, that is true in some cases but not in all cases.
> When red appears in a dream we have to consider the following:
> What kind of an object does it appear on?
> Which animal does it appear on?
> What is happening in the dream when this color is seen?

It is very important to remember and understand the situation your dream depicts when you see these colors because you may be experiencing one of the crucial warnings that come in a form of a dream.

The message imbedded in red may be intensified when the color is seen together with other colors at the same time.

Like red and white or black and red; or even red white and black in the same object.
The dreamer will have to combine the meanings of all these colors and make up one conclusion.

Some colors carry spiritual meanings so when they come together with red they bring a spiritual warning.
Red is a warm color therefore it carries messages of care and awareness. Depending on an object it appears on the meaning will be clearer through understanding object symbols.

> **Black**
Black is the color of the universe and the identity of the gods.

Black is a color which represents darkness and the opposite of the light. However within darkness there are elements which give birth to light.

Dreaming about dark colors is often associated with bad things; which is not entirely true.

Depending on the events in your dream such a dream may bring good or bad messages. Here also the objects or animals in your dream will have to be symbolically understood in order to decipher the meaning of the blackness in their depiction.

Remember that it is not always that darkness caries bad energy.

I have explained what the color black means in animals and some objects. Where clothes are concerned the black color is a sign of agony and grief.

Pay attention to who is wearing black in your dream and what they are doing. That will help to determine the nature of the message in your dream.

This color appears a lot in topics that are dealt with in other versions of The Oracle's Guide.

Follow the books and get more clarity on this color. For the sake of confusion I will not go deeper on this volume as the aim of this book is to enable the dreamer to interpret symbols using colors in them.

Just an understanding of darkness and the color black
will help the dreamer to interpret their symbols according
to their believes.

Black means different things in different believe systems,
so to avoid confusion we will not delve in the spiritual
side of the black color.

> **Green**
This color represents fertility, life and nature.
In a case where the color green appears in a dream one
should consider the natural elements of life, the renewal
of life where healing or nourishment is concerned and
birth of a new child.

Spiritually green is the color of healing and wellbeing, to
those who believe in luck it is a color of luck.
Green may also appear in animal, clothes or on any
object. The symbolism will always be of life, fertility and
healing as well as luck to those who believe in luck.
The events of your dream will tell what the color green
entails as a symbol.

Green plants are a symbol of life giving forces and
fertility.
Green animals are a symbol of birth or a new beginning,
the transformation of your soul and other life changing
events in your life.

- ➢ **Blue**

  Blue is the color of the sky or the color of the waters above; which many may be dubbed as a sign of heavens.

  When it comes to interpreting dreams with the color blue in them, one needs to hold an understanding of the cosmos and the other realms of existence.

  Blue is a highly charged color which has high spiritual significance.

  The color blue symbolizes the existence of cosmic beings in one's life.
  It also represents your spiritual guides.

  Any human who appears wearing blue in your dream represents your guides.

  Any object that appears in blue represents other dimensions which are interconnected with your reality.

  Pay attention to the people, animals and objects which appear in blue they have spiritual symbolism. Messages which are embedded in this color are of a spiritual nature and should be consciously interpreted as mistakes may lead a person astray.

  I will explain in detail the functions of a blue color in the spirit world in my next book about spiritual healing and self-healing.

This color also works as a symbol of healing.

> **White**
White is color of purity and light, it is the brightest color in existence. Religions use white as a symbol of holiness while spiritually the color white may represent one's soul.

But in dreams white can mean many different aspects according to where it appears and how it appears. White on an object represents the purity of such an object.

White on clothes represents the innocence and caring of the person wearing such. Your guides may appear wearing white, which would mean they are trying to show you the humbleness and the holiness of the person wearing white.

In a case where you are in the dark and stressing about life, white will appear as a color of comfort and hope. The light that shines in your future is often represented in white.

Everything that aluminate in white has a clear depiction of spirituality and higher consciousness.

- ➤ **Yellow**

  Yellow is the color of wisdom.
  It often appears as a symbol which reprimands, advice
  and enlighten the dreamer.

  It is also the color of prophecy which means such
  dreams where yellow appears is likely to come true.
  Anything that appears yellow in a dream symbolizes the
  prophecy behind the dream. The events of the dream will
  tell the interpreter what is being prophesied.
  Whoever appears wearing yellow in your dream will be
  your prophet or your Oracle in that dream.

- ➤ **Brown**

  Brown is a color of the ancestors; anything that appears
  brown in your dream symbolizes your ancestors.

  In a case where a dreamer is of different believes from
  those who believe in ancestors. The color brown will
  represent the reality of such a person. Which means; the
  way you see life and how you perceive your own reality
  will always appear in brown colors. Whether on objects
  or animals the color brown will symbolize your own
  reality. It will depict the realness and the truthfulness of
  your dream in terms of the message it carries.

  This also appears in natural dreams where the meaning is
  less significant to the dreamer's life.
  The spiritual side of this color symbol varies from culture
  to culture.

It would be in the best interest of the dreamer to compare the color to their believe systems and use such a believer to interpret their dream.

For those who believe in ancestors and spirit guides; indeed this color represents those spirits.

 Anything that appears in brown belongs to your guides and it is a message from them.

> **Other colors**
In a case where a dreamer encounters mixed colors or colors we did not mention in this book. That would require an artistic understanding of color shades, where the primary colors I mentioned are mixed to form such a color which appeared in one's dream. Then the meaning will be derived from the colors separately to form one deeper meaning of the color at hand.

If confusion arises still consult your Oracle for clarity. Bright colors represent the light and awareness or consciousness where else dark colors represent warnings and the depth of the situation in the dreamer's world.

Conclusion

Self-help is an easier way of approaching many difficulties in life, though from time to time we need extra help from outside. When we have the tools and mechanism to self-help we find it easier to pull through difficult situations. This version of The Oracle's Guide to dream interpretation serves as a guide to give you the first steps of self-helping. The guides that are listed in this volume are the basics of dream interpretation. When they are understood and practiced accordingly Dreamers will have no difficulties interpreting their dreams to see the meanings behind them. Unless the dream is more confusing to the dreamer but with the basics we provided here, it will be easier to understand the dreams and their meanings.

Every category explained in this book is connected to another, meaning that for one to be able to interpret their dreams efficiently, they will need to understand all categories and be a blue to connect them where necessary. For instance, in a case where the Dreamer encounters animals, objects and natural elements like water and trees; all of them appearing in one dream and in different colors. The Dreamer will have to consider the knowledge of all symbols and interpret each within the dream in order to reach the conclusion of the meaning of such a dream. Your Oracles will guide you and help you in terms of understanding the meanings of your dreams. However you would be having a clue as to what the dream meant given what you learned from this book.

I will continue to guide on the next volumes of The Oracle's Guide, keep contact with The Oracle or follow more books published on line and on shelves. Follow the Oracle on social media, your interaction will help in writing more Guides to your satisfaction.

Mpho Khoza

May the first light of creation shine upon all; with love and comfort from your guides and ancestors.

Ashe!!!

Volume 1 and volume 2

The oracle's Guide

Dream interpretation

Author Mpho Khoza

Release year 2022

www.ingramcontent.com/pod-product-compliance
Lightning Source LLC
Chambersburg PA
CBHW080941120726
48003CB00011B/3252